CONTINENTS OF THE WORLD

DISCOVERING

AUSTRALIA'S

LAND, PEOPLE, AND WILDLIFE

A MyReportLinks.com Book

Judy Alter

MyReportLinks.com Books

an imprint of

Enslow Publishers, Inc. E

Box 398, 40 Industrial Road
Berkeley Heights, NJ 07922
USA

MyReportLinks.com Books, an imprint of Enslow Publishers, Inc. MyReportLinks®
is a registered trademark of Enslow Publishers, Inc.

Library of Congress Cataloging-in-Publication Data

Alter, Judy, 1938–
  Discovering Australia's land, people, and wildlife / Judy Alter.
    p. cm. — (Continents of the world)
Summary: An introduction to the geography, history, economy, plants and
animals, culture, and people of the country that is also the world's
smallest continent.
Includes bibliographical references and index.
  ISBN 0-7660-5207-9
  1. Australia—Juvenile literature. [1. Australia.] I. Title. II.
Series.
  DU96.A49 2004
  994—dc22
                              2003016488

Printed in the United States of America

10 9 8 7 6 5 4 3 2 1

To Our Readers:
Through the purchase of this book, you and your library gain access to the Report Links that specifically back up this book.
The Publisher will provide access to the Report Links that back up this book and will keep these Report Links up to date on **www.myreportlinks.com** for three years from the book's first publication date.
We have done our best to make sure all Internet addresses in this book were active and appropriate when we went to press. However, the author and the Publisher have no control over, and assume no liability for, the material available on those Internet sites or on other Web sites they may link to.
The usage of the MyReportLinks.com Books Web site is subject to the terms and conditions stated on the Usage Policy Statement on **www.myreportlinks.com**.
A password may be required to access the Report Links that back up this book. The password is found on the bottom of page 4 of this book.
Any comments or suggestions can be sent by e-mail to comments@myreportlinks.com or to the address on the back cover.

Photo Credits: AP/Wide World Photos, p. 23; Artville, p. 1; © 1995–2003 Public Broadcasting Service (PBS), p. 25; © 1996–2003 National Geographic Society, pp. 15, 36; © 2003 National Geographic Society, p. 18; © Commonwealth of Australia 2003, Commonwealth Bureau of Meterorology (ABN 92 637 533 532), p. 11; © Corel Corporation, pp. 3, 12, 16, 20, 21, 26, 28, 30, 32, 39, 41, 43; © Tropical Savannas CRC, 1998, p. 14; Enslow Publishers, Inc., p. 9; MyReportLinks.com Books, p. 4; Photos.com, p. 35.

Cover Photo: Artville; Clipart.com.

Contents

About MyReportLinks.com Books

MyReportLinks.com Books
Great Books, Great Links, Great for Research!

The Report Links listed on the following four pages can save you hours of research time by **instantly** bringing you to the best Web sites relating to your report topic.

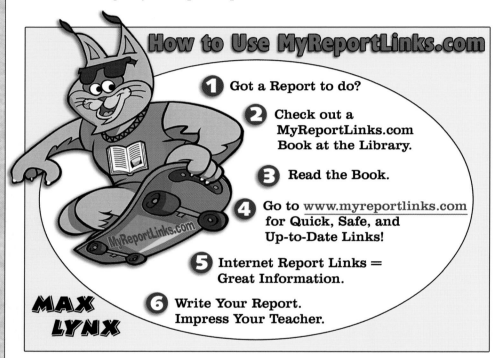

How to Use MyReportLinks.com

1. Got a Report to do?

2. Check out a MyReportLinks.com Book at the Library.

3. Read the Book.

4. Go to www.myreportlinks.com for Quick, Safe, and Up-to-Date Links!

5. Internet Report Links = Great Information.

6. Write Your Report. Impress Your Teacher.

MAX LYNX

The pre-evaluated Web sites are your links to source documents, photographs, illustrations, and maps. They also provide links to dozens—even hundreds—of Web sites about your report subject.

MyReportLinks.com Books and the MyReportLinks.com Web site save you time and make report writing easier than ever!

Please see "To Our Readers" on the copyright page for important information about this book, the MyReportLinks.com Web site, and the Report Links that back up this book. Please enter **CAU5489** if asked for a password.

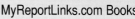
Report Links

 The Internet sites described below can be accessed at
http://www.myreportlinks.com

*Editor's Choice

▶*The World Factbook*: Australia

The CIA *World Factbook* Web site contains a profile on Australia which includes information about the country and continent's history and geography.

*Editor's Choice

▶Perry-Castañeda Library Map Collection: Maps of Australia and the Pacific

The Perry-Castañeda Library Map Collection Web site holds many maps of Australia including historical maps and strategic maps from World War II.

*Editor's Choice

▶Australian History

At the Australian History Web site you will learn about the first Australians, early exploration of the continent, European settlement, and much more.

*Editor's Choice

▶Australia: Through the *National Geographic* Lens

View images of Australia at this *National Geographic* Web site.

*Editor's Choice

▶Infoplease: Australia

Infoplease.com lets you research basic facts about Australia. Topics include government, history, and geography.

*Editor's Choice

▶Creature Feature: Koalas

The *National Geographic* Web site lists fun facts about the koala and contains a map of where they are located.

Report Links

The Internet sites described below can be accessed at http://www.myreportlinks.com

▶ **Another Hump on the Horizon: Ayers Rock**

At the *Smithsonian Magazine* Web site there is a brief article about the Ayers Rock in Australia.

▶ ***Australia: Beyond the Fatal Shores***

PBS' *Australia: Beyond the Fatal Shores* explores Australia's evolution into a modern nation.

▶ **Australia: Climate of Our Continent**

The Australia: Climate of Our Continent site provides online users with a climate outline, an overview of the climate in major cities, and explains how Australia compares with other continents.

▶ **Australia's Lost Kingdoms**

At Australia's Lost Kingdoms Web site you can explore the past 110 million years of Australian history, and learn about animals, fossils, and much more.

▶ **Australian War Memorial**

The Australian War Memorial Web site tells the stories of the memorial's history, and those who have been honored.

▶ **Boomerangs**

A brief history of the boomerang. There is even a section where you can learn how to make your own boomerang.

▶ **Culture and Recreation.gov.au**

Australia's history, culture, heritage, and much more are explained at the Culture and Recreation Web site.

▶ **Discovering Democracy: Australia**

Find out about Australia's government, and how it went from being a British colony to a Democratic nation.

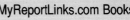
Report Links

The Internet sites described below can be accessed at http://www.myreportlinks.com

▶**Great Barrier Reef**
The Great Barrier Reef is located off the eastern coast of Australia. Read all about it.

▶*Kakadu: Australia's Ancient Wilderness*
PBS' *Kakadu: Australia's Ancient Wilderness* explores Australia's largest national park, Kakadu. The information focuses on the park's species and the native people of the area.

▶**Kip and Co.**
Explore Australia's wildlife: including the koala, kangaroo, bungarra, and many others.

▶**Lonely Planet: Australia**
At the Lonely Planet Web site you will find a brief overview of Australia where you will learn about the continent's attractions, history, culture, and much more.

▶**New South Wales Government**
The New South Wales Government Web site discusses this Australian state's economy, culture, environment, and much more.

▶**Northern Territory Government of Australia**
You can research government, economy, culture, and other topics of interest at the Northern Territory's official Web site.

▶**Queensland Government**
The area surrounding the waters of Queensland is home to some of the most interesting sea life in the world. Visit the Queensland Government Web site to find out about the tourism industry.

▶**South Australia**
The South Australia Web site contains facts about Australia's wildlife. Learn about mammals, birds, and reptiles: such as the kangaroo, glossy black cockatoo, and the blue-tongued lizard.

Report Links

The Internet sites described below can be accessed at http://www.myreportlinks.com

▶**South Australia Central**

On the South Australia Central Web site you will learn about community, government, environment, and much more.

▶**Tasmanian Devil**

The Tasmanian devil is a well-known animal. Learn about its habitat, physical features, breeding habits, diet, and more.

▶**Tasmania Online**

The Tasmania Online Web site takes a look at the state's business, government, and community.

▶**Tropical Savanna CRC**

On the Tropical Savanna CRC Web site you can research Australia's tropical savannas and the Tropical Savanna CRC's efforts to preserve this region.

▶**War & Peace Rationing and Rebuilding**

The War & Peace Rationing and Rebuilding Web site describes how life in Western Australia was during World War II.

▶**Welcome to Victoria**

Explore Victoria's government, culture, travel, natural beauty, and wildlife.

▶**Western Australia**

The Western Australia Web site contains information about its government, community, tourism, and much more.

▶**Wild World**

On this *National Geographic* Web site there are profiles about different areas in "Australasia" including the Australian Alps montane grasslands.

Australia Facts

Area*

2,967,893 square miles
7,686,850 square kilometers

Population (2002 Estimate)

18,972,350

Five Most Populous Cities

Sydney: 3,997,321
Melbourne: 3,366,542
Brisbane: 1,627,535
Perth: 1,339,993
Adelaide: 1,072,585

States and Territories

Australian Capital Territory
New South Wales
Northern Territory
Queensland
South Australia
Tasmania
Victoria
Western Australia

Highest Point

Mt. Kosciuszko
7,310 feet
2,228 meters

Lowest Point

Lake Eyre
52 feet below sea level
16 meters below sea level

Major Mountain Ranges

Australian Alps; MacDonnell Ranges

Major Lakes and Rivers

Rivers:
    Murray River, Darling River, Murrumbidgee River
Lakes:
    Lake Argyle, Lake Gordon, Lake Eyre, Lake Torrens, Lake Gairdner, Lake Frome

Major Religions

Most Australians are Christians. There are small Jewish and Islamic minorities. Some still celebrate Aboriginal religions.

Countries

Australia is the only country on the continent.

All metric measurements used in this text are approximate estimates.

Chapter 1

Down Under

Australia is the smallest of the world's seven continents. It has an area of 2,967,893 square miles (7,686,850 square kilometers)—about the size of the lower United States.[1] It is the only continent that is one country—the Commonwealth of Australia. One hundred fifty million years ago, Australia was part of a huge supercontinent, called Gondwanaland. This included Africa, South America, Antarctica, India, the Arabian Peninsula, and Australia. As the earth's crust shifted, Australia and Antarctica broke off together. About 65 million years ago, Australia broke off from Antarctica to become its own continent.

Australia means "southern land." The continent is south of the equator. The equator is an imaginary line around the middle of the earth that is equally distant from the North and South Poles. It divides the earth into the northern and southern hemispheres. The British commonly referred to Australia as "Down Under" and the name has stuck. This is because Australia is on the opposite side of the globe from Europe.

Australia's position south of the equator dictates the continent's climate. Its seasons are opposite those of the northern hemisphere. Summer begins in December or January and continues through April or May. July is actually the deepest part of winter.

Australia is home to over 19.5 million people.[2] The country has six official states—Tasmania (an island off

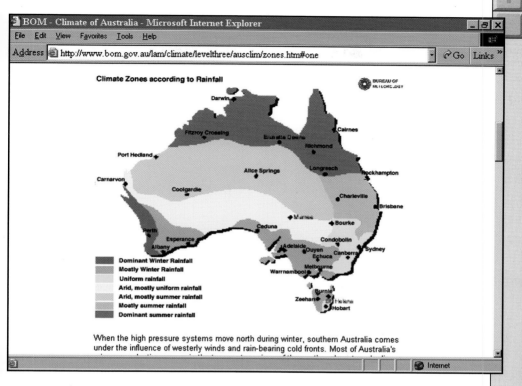

BOM - Climate of Australia - Microsoft Internet Explorer
File Edit View Favorites Tools Help
Address http://www.bom.gov.au/lam/climate/levelthree/ausclim/zones.htm#one   Go Links

Climate Zones according to Rainfall

BUREAU OF METEOROLOGY

Darwin

Fitzroy Crossing

Port Hedland

Carnarvon

Coolgardie

Alice Springs

Brunette Downs

Cairnes

Richmond

Longreach

Rockhampton

Charleville

Brisbane

Murrel

Bourke

Ceduna

Condoblin

Perth

Esperance

Albany

Adelaide

Ouyen

Echuca

Canberra

Sydney

Melbourne

Warrnambool

Burnie

Zeehan

Hobart

Dominant Winter Rainfall
Mostly Winter Rainfall
Uniform rainfall
Arid, mostly uniform rainfall
Arid, mostly summer rainfall
Mostly summer rainfall
Dominant summer rainfall

When the high pressure systems move north during winter, southern Australia comes under the influence of westerly winds and rain-bearing cold fronts. Most of Australia's

Internet

Australia is located far south of the equator. As a result, its climate is different from most places. This chart shows the rainy and dry parts of the continent.

the southeastern coast), Western Australia, South Australia, New South Wales, Victoria, and Queensland. It also has two territories, the Northern Territory and the Australian Capital Territory, which is home to Canberra, Australia's capital city. Eighty-eight percent of the population lives in cities.[3] Sydney is Australia's largest city. It is noted for its beautiful harbor. The dramatic opera house at the harbor's waterline is one of the most famous landmarks in the world.

Melbourne is the second largest city in the country and on the continent. It is the capital city of the state of Victoria, and is located on the southeastern coast of the

▲ *The Sydney Opera House is one of the most famous landmarks in the world. It opened in 1973.*

continent. The city is a major shipping port, and the area is known for its industrial strength. Automobiles, chemicals, clothing, food products, and machinery are among the chief products made there. People from over 140 different nations have made their home in Melbourne. The lifestyle of the city's residents reflects this blending of cultures.

Land and Climate

Australia is an arid, semitropical land.[1] The continent has three main land areas: the Eastern Highlands, the Central Lowlands, and the Western Plateau.

Highlands

The Eastern Highlands are a chain of mountains that run the length of the country, north to south, just inside the eastern coast. These mountains are called the Great Dividing Range because they divide the eastern strip from the much larger western portion of the continent. Australian mountains are not high compared to the Rocky Mountains or the Swiss Alps. Yet, within the Great Dividing Range there is a smaller range of mountains high enough to get snow in winter. These are called the Australian Alps, and they are popular for skiing.

The majority of Australia's population lives east of the Great Dividing Range. This area has the greatest rainfall and few temperature variations.

Central Lowlands and Western Plateau

The land immediately west of the mountains is known as the Central Lowlands. It is only a little over a thousand feet above sea level. The lowlands may have been a huge sea at one time. The Western Plateau is the largest area of the continent. Both the lowlands and the plateau are desert and semidesert, with sand dunes and small shrubs. The Western Plateau has three deserts—the Great Sandy,

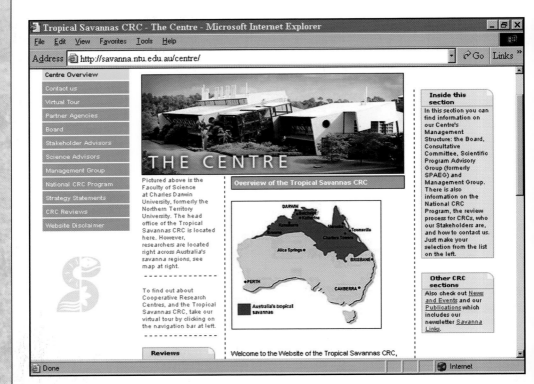

Tropical Savannas CRC - The Centre - Microsoft Internet Explorer

File Edit View Favorites Tools Help

Address http://savanna.ntu.edu.au/centre/   Go   Links

Centre Overview
Contact us
Virtual Tour
Partner Agencies
Board
Stakeholder Advisors
Science Advisors
Management Group
National CRC Program
Strategy Statements
CRC Reviews
Website Disclaimer

THE CENTRE

Pictured above is the Faculty of Science at Charles Darwin University, formerly the Northern Territory University. The head office of the Tropical Savannas CRC is located here. However, researchers are located right across Australia's savanna regions, see map at right.

To find out about Cooperative Research Centres, and the Tropical Savannas CRC, take our virtual tour by clicking on the navigation bar at left.

Overview of the Tropical Savannas CRC

DARWIN
Katherine
Kununurra
Broome
Mataranka
Townsville
Charters Towers
Alice Springs
BRISBANE
PERTH
CANBERRA

Australia's tropical savannas

Inside this section
In this section you can find information on our Centre's Management Structure: the Board, Consultative Committee, Scientific Program Advisory Group (formerly SPAEG) and Management Group. There is also information on the National CRC Program, the review process for CRCs, who our Stakeholders are, and how to contact us. Just make your selection from the list on the left.

Other CRC sections
Also check out News and Events and our Publications which includes our newsletter Savanna Links.

Reviews

Welcome to the Website of the Tropical Savannas CRC,

Done   Internet

▲ *Tropical savannas are among the many landforms found in Australia. Savannas are best described as wet, tropical grasslands.*

the Gibson, and the Great Victoria. The temperature is extremely hot during the day but cools rapidly at night in these deserts. At the edge of the deserts are grassland and savannas (wet, tropical grasslands). Australians call these grassy areas "the bush."

The Western Plateau has unusual outcroppings of rock. The most famous is Ayers Rock, now known by its Aboriginal name, Uluru. The Aborigine are Australia's native people. The world's biggest monolith or single piece of stone, it rises over eleven hundred feet (348 meters) from sandy scrubland, and is over two miles (3.6 kilometers) long. As much as two thirds of the rock may lie underground.[2]

The lowlands and the plateau are called the outback because they are "out back of" the Great Dividing Range. Roads are scarce and rough, and travelers must be prepared for emergencies.

▶ Australian Waters

The rivers and lakes of the outback are generally saltwater. In the dry season, they are beds of salt. Rainfall evaporates in the hot, dry air and cannot fill the rivers. Dry rivers have small ponds called billabongs. Lake Eyre is the largest lake in Australia. The largest river system, the Murray-Darling, provides water for cattle and crops.

Pictures: Australia by National Geographic (photos, wallpapers) - Microsoft Internet Explorer

File   Edit   View   Favorites   Tools   Help

Address 🔲 http://www.nationalgeographic.com/explorer/australia/abell/3.html   ⟳ Go   Links »

AUSTRALIA
THROUGH THE NATIONAL GEOGRAPHIC LENS

Two centuries of shifting dunes have exposed the thousands of limestone knobs that give Australia's Pinnacles Desert its name. Wind, rain, and sand sculpted the pinnacles—the main attractions of Namburg National Park. NEXT >>

Send this photo as an e-mail postcard!

<< Previous Image   Next Image >>

More on Australia at nationalgeographic.com

🔲 Done   🌐 Internet

▲ *The Pinnacles Desert is located in the state of Western Australia. The area is known for its wildflowers which are in bloom from August to October.*

▲ *Green Island is part of the state of Queensland, Australia. This area includes parts of the Great Barrier Reef, the largest coral reef in the world.*

Australia is surrounded by the Indian and South Pacific oceans and the Coral, Tasman, Arafura, and Timor seas. Its coastline consists of rocky cliffs, warm beaches, and muddy mangrove forests. Mangroves are trees that stand in water between land and open water. Australia's beaches offer surfing, sailing, parasailing, fishing, and other water activities. The beaches are important to Australia's tourist industry. Many of the coastal areas along these waters have coral reefs and unique sea animals.

▶ Coral Reefs

Coral reefs are made up of the skeletons of billions of tiny sea creatures. The Great Barrier Reef, off the coast of

Queensland, is the world's largest reef system. The reef stretches some 1,250 miles (2,011 kilometers). It is actually several reefs close together. At its southern end, the reef is 150 miles (241 kilometers) off the mainland. The northern end is closer to the coast and at places narrows to 10 miles (16.1 kilometers) in width. Tourists can view the reef through glass-bottom boats or the windows of semisubmersibles (submarines that hover just below the surface of the water). Snorkeling or scuba diving offers the best view.[3]

▶ Weather

Northern Australia is in the monsoon belt, where winds cause two kinds of weather: hot and dry, and hot and wet. In the summer, ocean winds bring rain, thunderstorms, and tropical disturbances. Temperatures remain relatively stable in summer and winter, but the summer humidity makes the temperature uncomfortable.[4] In Southern Australia, winters are cold but generally not freezing. Throughout the continent, there is little variation in temperature. Average temperatures are fairly mild. It is usually about 50°F or 10°C in winter; 70°F or 21°C in summer.

Australia is not noted for severe storms. Flood, fire, and dust storms are bigger problems. Rains come infrequently but can be extremely heavy when they do occur. Parched, dry land cannot absorb the water, and floods result. Fire is a danger because the land and its brush are generally very dry. The most common tree in Australia is the eucalyptus. It is an oily tree that feeds wildfires. In January 2003, the largest wildfire in a century threatened Canberra. Power was off in large portions of the city, and many people were evacuated.[5] Drought also encourages dust storms that pick up the dry, red dirt of the Western Plateau and hurl it into the urban areas to the east.

Chapter 3

People and Culture

The first Australians were a people known today as the Aborgine. They are believed to have come to Australia from Asia by boat or land bridge about fifty thousand years ago. A land bridge is a strip of land that connects two larger areas of land, such as two continents.

WORLD Magazine's Boomerangs! @ nationalgeographic.com - Microsoft Internet Explorer

File   Edit   View   Favorites   Tools   Help

Address   http://www.nationalgeographic.com/ngkids/0008/boomerang/index.html   Go   Links

NATIONALGEOGRAPHIC.COM
© 2003 National Geographic Society. All rights reserved.

SITE INDEX

BOOMERANGS!

Australians invented boomerangs long ago, but the modern sport of throwing them has caught on in the United States and other countries. Fans can find boomerangs of all shapes and sizes.

LEARN MORE >>

Internet

▲ *Aborigines developed the boomerang to help them hunt. When released correctly, a boomerang will return to the person who threw it.*

Aborigines

The first Aborigines lived in tribes, each with their own language. Men hunted land and sea animals using knives, spears, clubs, and nets made from grass and fiber. Aborigines developed the boomerang, a bent flat club that can be thrown so that it returns to its starting point. Women gathered vegetables, fruits, turtle and bird eggs, and small animals and fish. The only domestic animal was the dingo, a wolf-like dog. The dingo was sometimes used for transporting belongings.

The Aborigine did not have permanent housing. They were nomadic, moving from place to place in search of food. Sometimes they built huts of grasses or branches. They made clothing of furs and skins.[1]

European Settlement

The British were the first Europeans to settle in Australia. Captain James Cook explored the continent and claimed it for Great Britain in 1770. The first British settlement was established in 1788. From 1788 until 1852, England used Australia as a penal colony. The residents were convicts and the soldiers who supervised them. In that period of time, the British sent over 168,000 convicts to Australia. Few returned to Great Britain after completing their sentences. The population of Australia was entirely British and Aborigine. For the most part, it remained that way until the middle of the twentieth century.

After World War II (1939–45), the Australian government developed a program to attract immigrants. This was part of a plan to strengthen the country's economy and defenses. Called "Populate or Perish," it was believed that by increasing the population the Australians would be better

▲ *The Aborigines were the first known Australians. This man is a modern-day Aborigine elder.*

able to defend themselves against neighboring countries. Between 1947 and 1968, eight hundred thousand non-British immigrants settled in Australia. In the 1970s, immigration from Southeast Asia increased greatly.[2]

▶ British Influence

In spite of non-British immigration, the basic culture of Australia still follows a British model. English is the language of the country by custom, but not by law. Even Australian religion is influenced by the British. Anglicanism (the English Protestant Church) and Catholicism are the dominant religions. The country's government is a parliamentary democracy like that of England, with an upper house and a lower house.

Government

The upper house, called the Senate, has seventy-six members—twelve from each of the six states and two each from the two territories. The lower house, the House of Representatives, has 150 members, each representing an electoral division. Representatives serve three-year terms.[3]

The governor-general appoints the prime minister. The prime minister is the leader of the party holding the majority of seats in the House of Representatives. Elections are held every three years. However, if the prime minister's party loses control, all officials offer their resignations, and parliament is dissolved. A new election is held.[4]

The Australian cabinet consists of the prime minister, the treasurer, the minister of foreign affairs, and other selected ministers.[5]

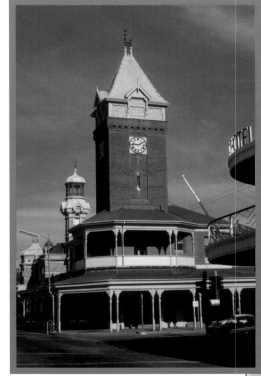

As in the United States, each state has a legislature, also called a parliament. In addition, each state has its own system of local governments to handle roads, health and safety, land-use controls, etc.

The town of Broken Hill is home to some of the main Australian silver and lead mines.

▶ Education

State governments control most aspects of education. Australia has the usual primary and secondary levels of schools. At the third level, students may go to a university, pursue technical education, or seek private education to prepare for business, secretarial, computer positions, etc. Education in the territories is the responsibility of the commonwealth government.

At the university level, a postgraduate diploma, master's, and doctorate degrees may follow a three-year bachelor's degree. Australian universities consistently rank within the top fifty universities in the Asia-Pacific region. Three business schools rank within the top ten in the region. Universities are created by an act of parliament and are accredited by the government, which maintains close supervision over the quality of education.

▶ G'day Mate

In spite of its close ties to Britain, Australia has developed its own distinctive culture. Even the language differs. The most common greeting in Australia is "G'day," a spirited shortening of the British "Good day." Australians speak of throwing meat on the "barbie" (barbecue) and talk of going on a "walkabout," an extended hiking trip through the bush. Friends are often called "mate." The origins of that phrase may trace back to the shipment of convicts when people were shipmates. Australians call fellowship, "mateship."

▶ Literature

Australia has its own literary tradition. In its earliest colonial days, the principal writing was journalism. In the twentieth century, authors of prose, poetry, and drama shaped a body of literature that speaks of Australian culture. P. L. Travers, author of the Mary Poppins books, is an Australian. Patrick White, author of *Voss* and *The Eye of the Storm*, among other titles, is Australia's only Nobel Prize winner for literature. Thomas Keneally won Britain's Booker Prize for his novel, *Schindler's Ark*. *My Brother Jack*, by George Johnston, covers the period from World War I to World War II.

Australian Film Industry

The country also has a thriving film industry and has produced some movies that have become international classics. The movie *Crocodile Dundee* was written by Australian Paul Hogan. He also starred in this film about the New York City adventures of a crocodile hunter from the outback.

Nicole Kidman is one of the most famous Australian actresses. In 2003, the Academy of Motion Picture Arts & Sciences awarded her an Oscar for best actress for her work in the movie The Hours.

Other classic Australian films include *Breaker Morant.* Released in 1980, it is about three Australian junior officers tried for murder during the Boer War in Africa. The movie is based on fact and portrays the fate of one of Australia's bush poets, an officer named Breaker Morant. *The Man from Snowy River* (1982) tells the story of a young mountain boy who joins experienced stockmen in pursuit of a runaway horse. The story is based on a poem by Banjo Paterson, who was known for ballads that captured the spirit of the outback.

American movie stars who grew up in Australia include Russell Crowe, Mel Gibson, and Nicole Kidman.

▶ Leisure

Australians enjoy many recreational activities. The Melbourne Cup is the country's most famous horse race. If they cannot be there, Australians will turn on the "telly" or television, to watch the race. Tennis is an important sport in the country, and Australia has produced many championship tennis players. Australia is also known for Australian rules football, a game that combines the rules of American football with the sport of rugby. The national pasttime, however, is the sport of cricket.

Every year on January 26, the country celebrates Australia Day. On January 26, 1788, Captain Arthur Phillip took formal possession of the continent for Britain and became its first governor. The celebration, begun in 1838, was called Foundation Day for many years. There are formal ceremonies such as flag raisings, citizenship ceremonies, and community awards.[6]

For more lively entertainment, the mountain ranges offer skiing and rock climbing. Australian beaches offer sailing, surfing, and scuba diving.

Chapter 4 ▶

Animal and Plant Life

Because it was isolated by water from other continents for so long, Australia has unique animal and plant life. Its indigenous animals were unable to wander to other lands, as has happened, for instance, in North and South America. Plant seeds and roots were not carried by wind as on other continents.

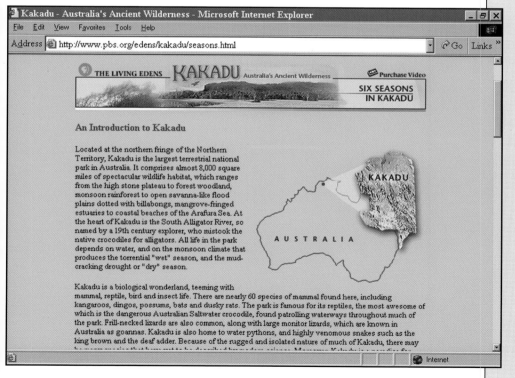

Kakadu - Australia's Ancient Wilderness - Microsoft Internet Explorer

File   Edit   View   Favorites   Tools   Help

Address 🔘 http://www.pbs.org/edens/kakadu/seasons.html   ▾   ⟳ Go   Links »

THE LIVING EDENS   **KAKADU**   *Australia's Ancient Wilderness*   📹 Purchase Video

SIX SEASONS
IN KAKADU

An Introduction to Kakadu

Located at the northern fringe of the Northern Territory, Kakadu is the largest terrestrial national park in Australia. It comprises almost 8,000 square miles of spectacular wildlife habitat, which ranges from the high stone plateau to forest woodland, monsoon rainforest to open savanna-like flood plains dotted with billabongs, mangrove-fringed estuaries to coastal beaches of the Arafura Sea. At the heart of Kakadu is the South Alligator River, so named by a 19th century explorer, who mistook the native crocodiles for alligators. All life in the park depends on water, and on the monsoon climate that produces the torrential "wet" season, and the mud-cracking drought or "dry" season.

KAKADU

AUSTRALIA

Kakadu is a biological wonderland, teeming with mammal, reptile, bird and insect life. There are nearly 60 species of mammal found here, including kangaroos, dingos, possums, bats and dusky rats. The park is famous for its reptiles, the most awesome of which is the dangerous Australian Saltwater crocodile, found patrolling waterways throughout much of the park. Frill-necked lizards are also common, along with large monitor lizards, which are known in Australia as goannas. Kakadu is also home to water pythons, and highly venomous snakes such as the king brown and the deaf adder. Because of the rugged and isolated nature of much of Kakadu, there may

▲ Kakadu is the largest national park in Australia. Many of Australia's endangered animals are protected here.

▶ Animal Life

Australia is home to two unusual species of mammals. These are the marsupials and monotremes. Marsupials are animals that carry their young in a pouch. The newborn, not yet fully formed, claws its way from its mother's body to her pouch and feeds from a nipple there. Kangaroos are the most familiar marsupials. A newborn kangaroo is called a joey. Kangaroos' powerful hind legs and long muscular tails, give them the ability to move at high speeds.

Australia has about fifty species of kangaroos and wallabies (a small kangaroo). They are also known as macropods (big-footed) and are found on all parts of the continent. For instance, rock-wallabies and common wallaroos (reddish-gray kangaroos) live in caves, while tropical tree-kangaroos sleep in the rain forest canopy. They generally live in large groups, called mobs.[1]

The wombat is a nocturnal, burrowing marsupial about the size of a badger. It lives on herbs and, like the kangaroo, can move at amazing speeds. Horsemen

◀ A close-up of an Australian kangaroo. These marsupials are found on all parts of the continent.

in the mountains are careful of wombat holes that can trip a human or a horse.

Tasmanian devils found only on the island of Tasmania are carnivorous or meat-eating marsupials. These predators eat large corpses from the inside out. They usually forage at night, alone. Their teeth are strong enough to kill a victim and then destroy all evidence of their feast.

The koala, a national symbol of Australia, is also a marsupial. Found mostly on the southeastern coast, it lives in eucalyptus trees. Young koalas, out of their mother's pouch, often cling to her back. Although they look cuddly, they generally do not want attention from people.

The second species unique to Australia is the monotreme. These are warm-blooded animals that lay eggs but still nurse their young. One example is the platypus, a furry mammal with snake-like characteristics. It is recognizable by its duckbill and large feet. The rubbery duckbill helps the platypus search for edible organisms in the water. Platypuses eat at night in the streams of the eastern mainland and Tasmania.

The echidna is another monotreme. It is a spiny creature about 14 to 21 inches (35.5 to 53.3 centimeters) long. When threatened, the echidna rolls into a spiny ball, much like a porcupine.

▷ A Mythical Creature

The bunyip is a solitary animal said to be a cross between a duck and a brown bear. It is supposed to look a little like a platypus. Bunyips allegedly feast at night and dig burrows in dead-end river channels. There are no documented sightings of bunyips, yet some people feel certain that they exist.

Koalas have become a national symbol of Australia.

Birds

Among the birds found on the Australian continent are magpies, lyrebirds, bowerbirds, little penguins (the world's smallest), cockatoos, and kookaburras. The kookaburra, or Australian kingfisher, has a loud cry that sounds like a laugh; it is sometimes called the laughing jackass. The male bowerbird decorates its nest, or bower, with berries, flowers, feathers, moss, and anything else bright it can find. Then it tries to attract a female to its beautiful nest. Australia also has flightless birds such as emu and cassowary.

Reptiles

Australia has about 500 species of lizards, 130 species of snakes, and two species of crocodiles. The crocodiles found in the north are either "freshies" (freshwater) or "salties" (saltwater). The saltwater crocodile is the world's largest, sometimes weighing over a ton. Freshies are small and are no threat to humans.[2]

Sea Life

Australia's coastlines, bays, inlets, and reefs are home to a wide variety of marine life. Dugongs, or sea cows, graze on sea grasses and mangroves in the tropical and semitropical waters to the north. In most coastal waters, dolphins swim playfully alongside boats, and sea lions charge up to boats and then plunge deep underwater to twist away. Humpback whales migrate along the east coast, going north in the fall to mate in the warmer waters and returning south in the spring.

Australia's reefs, including the Great Barrier Reef, are ecologically rich. Colorful fish live on these reefs, from fairy basslets to potato cod. Four thousand types of mollusks (clams, snails, etc.) also live there, along with sea urchins, sea anemones, starfish, sea cucumbers, shrimp, crabs, and many species of sponge. Dangerous inhabitants include venomous scorpions and stinging jellyfish. Whale sharks, a large but fairly gentle fish that does not threaten people, also live in the waters around reefs, especially the Ningaloo Reef on the northwest corner of the continent.[3]

▷ Animals and the Land

Domesticated animals, introduced by European settlers, disturb the natural balance of Australia's ecology. Cattle and sheep destroy water holes. Rabbits brought from England for hunting have multiplied until there are now millions of wild rabbits. They compete with native animals, particularly the bilby (a rabbit-like marsupial) for food. Rabbits' rapid consumption of grass also leads to soil erosion. The government has tried various programs to control rabbits, including trapping and poisoning them.

The English also brought foxes to hunt, as well as cats. The cats were brought as companions or to hunt mice. These have multiplied in the wild, particularly because they feed on rabbits. In New South Wales, farmers brought in toads to control the grubs (caterpillars) that were

destroying sugar cane crops. The toads have now spread throughout New South Wales and eastern Queensland. Even kangaroos are multiplying and becoming a serious nuisance. They are unafraid of people and show up in cities in alarming numbers.

Dingoes, the wild dogs that followed the Aborigines to the continent, have also become a problem for some. A dingo can kill fifty sheep in one night. In an effort to keep the dingoes out of sheep-grazing lands, Australians built the world's largest fence. The Wild Dog Fence stands 6 feet high (1.8 meters) and runs some 3,700 miles (5,530 kilometers) across the southeastern corner of the states of South Australia, New South Wales, and Queensland.[4] Unfortunately, it is difficult to maintain and has many holes in it. Dingoes have also been known to dig under the fence.

▲ *Dingoes are wild dogs that have been on the Australian continent since Aboriginal times. Farmers have to be sure that dingoes do not attack their sheep.*

▶ Plant Life

Australia does not have large, dense forests. Generally, plant growth consists of grasslands, shrubs, or open forests. The eucalyptus, often called a "gum," is an evergreen hardwood with tough, thick leaves that resist water loss. There are five hundred species of eucalyptus. Shrub land is covered with tropical plants and trees, such as the locust tree. Many of Australia's plants are drought resistant. They have deep taproots and great root density so they can find water in the ground. Shiny plant surfaces reflect the sun's rays rather than absorbing them.[5]

The Eastern Highlands region has both temperate and tropical rain forests. (Temperate zones have seasonal variations; tropical zones are always hot.) Tropical rain forests are found in the north, closer to the equator. These forests have tall trees and several layers of plants. They are home to colorful birds and several species of possum. There are no monkeys, which are generally found in rain forests throughout the world.

Since English colonization of Australia, the continent has lost 70 percent of its native vegetation, 45 percent of its total forest, and 75 percent of its rain forests. Today, land clearing continues at a rate greater than that in the Amazon Basin. The loss of this plant growth has meant that 23 percent of mammals, 9 percent of birds, and 9 percent of freshwater fish are extinct or endangered. The same is true for 7 percent of reptiles, 16 percent of amphibians, and 5 percent of the plant species. Clear-cutting also increases the saline (salt) level in rivers, further endangering living organisms in the rivers. The government has resolved to protect 95 percent of the remaining old-growth forests from clearing.[6]

Economy

Australia is a relatively wealthy country. Most of its wealth comes from mining and manufacturing. Australia has extensive mineral deposits and mines iron ore, bauxite (used in making aluminum), oil, and nickel. Its major exports include natural gas and mining products, such as iron and steel. The country's most important export is wool, mostly from merino sheep, and it has a thriving textile industry. Australia is also the world's largest exporter of beef. Most of its exports go to Asia. Australia was active in forming the Asia-Pacific Economic Cooperation (APEC) that seeks to further interests of Pacific nations.[1]

▲ Boats sailing in St. George's Bay, by the town of St. Helens, Tasmania. Commercial fishing and the protection of water culture are important to the Australian economy.

Fishing

Commercial fishing is an important Australian industry. The country has one of the largest fishing areas in the world. Rock lobster, abalone, bluefin tuna, pink snapper, shark, scallops, prawns, and crab are some of the seafood caught in Australian waters. Australia is a world leader in protecting birds and sharks from accidental entanglement in fishing nets and lines. The country also protects its water culture by controlling the number and size of fishing boats, the type of equipment used, the length of the season, and the number of fish caught.

Forestry

Similarly, Australia has taken steps in recent years to protect its native forests. A small portion of these forests is harvested each year. The forestry industry harvests trees for timber and such wood products as paper, cardboard, and furniture. Many of these products are exported.

Tourism

Tourism has become increasingly important in Australia. The country offers visitors a wide variety of sports activities. It also offers sophisticated cities, such as Sydney and Melbourne, or "roughing it" tours of the outback. An estimated 5 million tourists visit the country each year.[2]

Service industries are a large part of the continent's economy. These industries include hotels, transportation, financial institutions, energy supplies, and others that serve the needs of both residents and tourists.

Australia is also becoming increasingly well-known for its wines, which are exported throughout the world.

Chapter 6

History

Portuguese sailors in the first half of the 1500s are believed to be the first Europeans to sight Australia, but they left no records. In the 1640s, the Dutch East India Company sent Abel Tasman on two voyages. In 1642, he landed on the island now called Tasmania. He had called it Van Diemen's Land. It would be renamed after him nearly two hundred years later to remove the stigma of the penal colony that had once been there.[1]

A pirate named William Dampier visited Australia in 1688 and 1698 and made some onshore exploration. He reported that the country was so dismal that it should be forgotten.[2]

▶ Great Britain Stakes Its Claim

In 1768, Captain James Cook led a scientific expedition to Tahiti and other parts of the Pacific Ocean. On April 19, 1770, his ship, the *Endeavour*, came within sight of the extreme southeastern tip of Australia. Cook followed the coast north, looking for a place to go ashore. Nine days later, he found an opening in the cliffs and landed at a harbor he called Botany Bay. The scientists on board *Endeavour* went ashore and recorded detailed descriptions of plants, animals, and birds. They also sighted Aborigines but did not make contact with them. Cook recorded that they did not seem friendly.

The *Endeavour* followed the coast north but was damaged on a reef off Queensland. Cook was forced to establish

Abel Tasman explored parts of ▶
Australia for the Dutch East
India Company. The state of
Tasmania is named after him.

a small settlement for six
weeks while repairs were
made. Then he and his
crew continued north,
rounding the York
Peninsula at the northeast corner of the continent. They
went ashore, and Cook planted the Union Jack (the flag
of Great Britain) and claimed the land for King George III
of England.

British settlement of the land came within twenty years
of Cook's exploration. After the American Revolution,
Britain could no longer send convicts to North America to
ease the overcrowding in its jails. In 1786, King George III
decided to send convicts to Botany Bay in Australia. Captain
Arthur Phillip arrived in 1788 with a fleet of eleven ships,
holding 1,030 people, livestock, and supplies for two years.
Of the people, 548 men and 188 women were convicts
under sentence of deportation from England.[3] Phillip eventually settled his people at Port Jackson (near present-day
Sydney). He became the first governor of Australia. Phillip
completely overlooked the presence of the Aborigines and
declared the land unoccupied. Britain colonized it as
unoccupied land. That concept would be important in
twentieth-century dealings with the Aborigines.

A second fleet from Britain arrived in Australia in 1790, and a third in 1791. Australia then had a British population of about four thousand.[4]

▶ Convicts

Life was hard for the convicts. They were mostly minor criminals—pickpockets, prostitutes, petty thieves, and sheep stealers. Because crops had not begun to yield enough food, the colony was dependent on supplies from England. People lived in fear of starvation if a ship sank or some other disaster struck. Most knew they would never return to England.

▲ The city of Perth is located on the Australia's west coast, along the Indian Ocean. Perth was one of the first Australian settlements.

Phillip believed that Australia had to attract settlers if it was to prosper. He began to grant land to officers, soldiers, and emancipists (convicts who had served their time). When he returned to Great Britain, his second-in-command, Major Francis Grose, continued the practice. The officers had plenty of land, lots of money, and cheap labor. They made huge profits at the expense of the few small farmers, mostly emancipists.

In 1806, William Bligh, who had survived a mutiny on his ship, the *Bounty*, was governor. In what was called the Rum Rebellion, the rebel soldiers arrested Bligh. When word of the rebellion reached England, King George III sent Lieutenant Colonel Lachlan Macquarie with a military regiment to take over. The soldiers who had abused their privileges were called back to England.

Among those sent back to England was a man named John Macarthur. He had introduced merino sheep to Australia. His wife stayed and raised the sheep when he was sent back to England, and he is credited with being the father of Australia's wool industry.[5]

Macquarie soon gave emancipated convicts the rights of citizens and appointed them to public positions. The practice of transportation of convicts to Australia from England was discontinued in 1852.

▶ Settlement

Settlement of Australia was slow. In 1800, there were only two settlements—Sydney Cove and Norfolk Island, both penal colonies. The first settlement in Tasmania, Hobart, also started as a penal colony. Gradually settlements were established at Melbourne, Perth, Adelaide, and Brisbane. The continent, however, was not thoroughly explored until the 1860s. The first overland telegraph was strung in 1872.[6]

▷ Gold Rush

Settlement of Victoria was given a great boost in 1852 with the discovery of a large amount of gold near the town of Ballarat. Gold had been found there before, but only in small quantities. By law, the gold belonged to the government, so these small discoveries were ignored. The Ballarat discovery soon caused a gold rush. The government was forced to give up the law of ownership. Instead, it instituted a monthly fee for a diggers' license. The government made money whether gold was found or not. Soon there were diggings all over Victoria.[7]

Word of the gold rush spread. Migrants came from Ireland, Scotland, England, Europe, and the Americas. Chinese migrants came as well, to dig for gold and to raise and sell market goods to the miners. The European population, however, resented the Asian immigrants, and there were race riots. These set the stage for a fear of Asia that gripped Australia until the late twentieth century.

The gold rush became part of Australian folklore as the English, Scots, and Irish created songs and wrote about life at the diggings, the gold towns, squatters with their sheep and cattle stations, swagmen (Australian for hobos), and bushrangers (outlaws in the isolated bush country). Many bushrangers became folk heroes, just as some outlaws have become heroes in the United States.

Few people made fortunes from the Australian gold rush. Many who came to mine the gold eventually stayed to farm. The population increased. The Industrial Revolution in England had created a market for Australia's mineral and agricultural raw materials. This improved the Australian economy.

▲ *This area is a Tiwi Aboriginal "Pukamani" grave site. It is located on Australia's Melville Island.*

▶ Aborigines

The Aborigines were a concern for the government. At the time of British settlement, they had no central government, no permanent settlement, and no concept of ownership of the land. They spoke 250 languages and could not communicate with each other.[8] It was impossible for them to make a coordinated resistance to European settlement.

The Europeans drove them from their land and brought diseases such as smallpox, measles, pneumonia, and tuberculosis. They cut down forests and introduced new animals. By 1860, there were 20 million sheep in Australia. Sheep and cattle destroyed water holes and ruined the habitat of the animals that the Aborigines hunted. Starving natives speared English cattle. The guilty

were generally caught and killed. For the first hundred years of European settlement, few Europeans were prosecuted for killing Aborigines.

Some Aborigines developed guerrilla warfare tactics. They had superior numbers and weapons. The British had only unreliable flintlocks (a type of rifle), which were difficult and slow to reload. Aborigines could throw spears faster than the British could fire. When the settlers got repeating rifles, they crushed armed Aborigine resistance. By the 1880s, only a few small groups of Aborigines in the far outback were untouched by European settlement.[9]

In the early 1860s, the Board for Protection of Aborigines put surviving natives on six reservations. These were farming communities run by Christian missionaries. The missionaries would try to convert the natives to Christianity as they worked the land.

In 1866, the Aborigine Protection Act forced those under thirty-one to leave the reserves in an attempt to make them blend into European culture. Families were broken up. By 1923, there were only two reserves. It seemed that the problems facing the Aborigine were not close to being solved.[10]

▷ Independence From Great Britain

In the early 1890s, Australians began to discuss breaking free from British control. Unlike the American Revolution, Australia's separation was accomplished peacefully. Independence required that the colonies agree on a constitution. In addition, the voters had to support the move, and Britain had to agree. Britain fully supported Australian independence. In July 1900, the British Parliament passed the Commonwealth of Australia Constitution Act. The Australian constitution established a federal parliament,

An Anzac Day celebration at *the town hall in Sydney, Australia. People from all over Australia celebrate Anzac Day every April 25.*

set up a high court, and transferred some powers from state to federal control. It did not specify the functions of the state governments, though. On January 1, 1901, the governor-general proclaimed the new Commonwealth of Australia in ceremonies in Centennial Park in Sydney.

Australia did not completely cut its ties to Britain. The queen retained rule over the land. Australia considered itself a British and/or European outpost. In 1901, the Immigration Restriction Bill was passed, requiring that prospective citizens take a dictation test in a European language. The bill was designed to keep out Asians and Pacific Islanders. The test was not abolished until 1958.

World War I

When World War I broke out in Europe in 1914, Australian troops fought alongside the British. At the time, Australia had voluntary military service. Conscription (a draft) was suggested, but the voters defeated it. Over 300,000 Australians served in the war, and over 60,000 were killed. ANZACs (members of the Australian and New

Zealand Army Corps) were cited for their bravery. Anzac Day, April 25, commemorates the Australian soldiers killed at Gallipoli in 1915 in a British attempt to open the Dardanelles (a strip of water separating Europe from Turkey and Asia Minor—Gallipoli is on Turkish land).

The Great Depression

The Great Depression hit Australia hard. Prices for wool and wheat, its two main exports, dropped dramatically. By 1931, one third of the heads of households were unemployed. Poverty spread across the country. Swagmen were common. Recovery began as early as 1933 when prices began to rise.[11]

United States Ally

When World War II came, Australia again sent men to fight alongside British troops, mostly in New Guinea. Australia was afraid Japan would attack. After the December 7, 1941 bombing of American ships at Pearl Harbor, national defense took priority for Australia. When the British called for more troops, Australian Prime Minister John Curtin refused, saying they were needed in the Pacific. United States troops helped protect Australia by defeating the Japanese at the Battle of the Coral Sea. This victory began a shift in Australian loyalty from Britain to the United States of America. Today the country is very Americanized.[12]

Australians fought alongside United States troops in Korea. The government joined the Southeast Asia Treaty Organization and instituted the Colombo Pact of 1950, which joined nations to stop the spread of communism in Southeast Asia. In 1965, Australia sent troops to Vietnam, but many Australian citizens did not support this war. In

1972, the Labour Party, under Gough Whitlam, withdrew the troops from Vietnam.[13] Australian troops also aided the United States in 2003 during Operation Iraqi Freedom.

▷ Plight of the Aborigine

Also in 1972, the Australian government adopted a policy of self-determination for the Aborigines. In the early 1900s, legislation had further segregated the natives, putting restrictions on their right to own property and seek employment. The government controlled where they could live, whom they could marry, and whether or not they could raise their children. If authorities suspected a non-Aborigine fathered a child, the child was taken from its Aborigine mother.[14]

▲ Australia has many wide-open areas including the deserts and the outback, but there are also modern cities. This is a view of the city of Sydney, north from the Centrepoint Tower.

In 1976, the Lands Right Act, effective only in the Northern Territory, set a precedent for return of land to the Aborigines. It overturned the concept of unoccupied land, under which Britain had claimed the continent. The act established Aboriginal land councils that could claim land for traditional owners. However, it set many restrictions on what land could be reclaimed. Since then, many lawsuits seeking return of land have been brought in several Australian states. There has been only a limited return of land.

▶ Modern-Day Australia

In the early twenty-first century, Australia's sophisticated cities stand in sharp contrast to the outback. The outback is still some of the most rugged, unsettled terrain in the world. Life in these areas is very different. The cities, on the other hand, are huge urban centers.

Australia faces social problems, such as racial injustice, and environmental problems, such as flood, fire, and the abuse of its natural resources. It is a country and continent, though, which is working on its problems with fiercely loyal citizens who are proud to be "Aussies."

Chapter Notes

Chapter 1. Down Under

1. Thomas L. McKnight, *Australia's Corner of the World: A Geographical Summation* (Englewood Cliffs, N.J.: Prentice-Hall, Inc., 1970), p. 22.

2. Paul Harding, et al., *Australia: A Lonely Planet Australia Guide* (Hawthorn, Victoria, Australia: Lonely Planet Publications, 2002), p. 56.

3. Ibid., p. 50.

Chapter 2. Land and Climate

1. Thomas L. McKnight, *Australia's Corner of the World: A Geographical Summation* (Englewood Cliffs, N.J.: Prentice-Hall, Inc., 1970), p. 29.

2. Paul Harding, et al., *Australia: A Lonely Planet Australia Guide* (Hawthorn, Victoria, Australia: Lonely Planet Publications, 2002), p. 414.

3. Ibid., pp. 500–501.

4. McKnight, p. 30.

5. "Residents gird to flee wildfires in Canberra," *Fort Worth Star-Telegram*, January 21, 2003, 5A.

Chapter 3. People and Culture

1. R. L. Heathcote, *Australia* (Essex England: Longman Scientific & Technical, 1994), pp. 13, 55, 57, 59.

2. Mark Armstrong, *Victoria: a Lonely Planet Australia Guide* (Hawthorn, Victoria, Australia: Lonely Planet Publications, 1996), p. 21.

3. Commonwealth of Australia, "Parliament An Overview," Parliament of Australia Education, September 18, 2003, <http://www.aph.gov.au/parl.htm> (December 4, 2003).

4. Ruth Atkins and Adam Graycar, *Governing Australia* (Sydney: John Wiley & Sons Australia PTY, Ltd., 1972), p. 65.

5. Ibid., p. 67.

6. James Walter, ed., *Australian Studies: A Survey* (New York: Oxford University Press, 1989), p. 18.

Chapter 4. Animal and Plant Life

1. Paul Harding, et al., *Australia: A Lonely Planet Australia Guide* (Hawthorn, Victoria, Australia: Lonely Planet Publications, 2002), p. 39.

2. Ibid., p. 43.

3. Ibid., p. 45.

4. Australian Tourist Commission, "Offbeat Facts," About Australia, 2003, <http://www.australia.com/about_australia/facts_and_figures.../Facts1_ALL.aust?L=en&C=U> (December 4, 2003).

5. Thomas L. McKnight, *Australia's Corner of the World: A Geographical Summation* (Englewood Cliffs, N.J.: Prentice-Hall, Inc., 1970), pp. 36–37.

6. Harding, pp. 50–51.

Chapter 5. Economy

1. Paul Harding, et al., *Australia: A Lonely Planet Australia Guide* (Hawthorn, Victoria, Australia: Lonely Planet Publications, 2002), p. 56.

2. Ibid., p. 57.

Chapter 6. History

1. Paul Harding, et al., *Australia: A Lonely Planet Australia Guide* (Hawthorn, Victoria, Australia: Lonely Planet Publications, 2002), p. 22.

2. Ibid.

3. Ibid., p. 23.

4. Ibid.

5. Ibid., p. 24.

6. Ibid., p. 26.

7. Ibid., p. 27.

8. Ibid.

9. Ibid.

10. Mark Armstrong, *Victoria: a Lonely Planet Australia Guide* (Hawthorn, Victoria, Australia: Lonely Planet Publications, 1996), p. 20.

11. Harding, p. 29.

12. Armstrong, p. 20.

13. Harding, p. 31.

14. City of Sydney, "Government Policy in Relation to Aboriginal People," Barani, 2002, <http://www.cityofsydney.nsw.gov.au/barani/themes/theme3.htm> (December 15, 2003).

Further Reading

Banting, Erinn. *Australia, the Land* (Lands, Peoples & Cultures). New York: Crabtree Publishers, 2002.

Darlington, Robert A. *Australia.* Austin, Tex.: Raintree Publishers, 2000.

Dolce, Laura. *Australia.* Broomall, Penn.: Chelsea House Publishers, 1999.

Finley, Carol. *Aboriginal Art of Australia: Exploring Cultural Traditions.* Minneapolis: Lerner Publishing Group, 1998.

Griffiths, Diana. *Australia.* Milwaukee, Wis.: Gareth Stevens Pub., 1999.

Hill, Valerie. *Australia.* Broomall, Penn.: Mason Crest Publishers, 2002.

Israel, Fred L. and Arthur M. Schlesinger, Jr. *Australia: The Unique Continent.* Broomall, Penn.: Chelsea House Publishers, 1999.

Sammis, Fran. *Australia and The South Pacific.* Tarrytown, N.Y.: Benchmark Books, 2000.

Sayre, April Pulley. *Australia.* Brookfield, Conn.: Millbrook Press, Incorporated, 1998.

Sharp, Anne Wallace. *Australia.* San Diego, Calif.: Lucent Books, 2003.

Somervill, Barbara. *Australia.* Chanhassen, Minn.: Child's World, 2004.

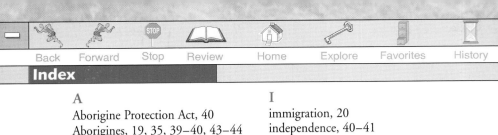
Index